MW01101508

INVISIBLE WORLDS

Exploring the Past

Anita Croy

 **Marshall Cavendish**
Benchmark
New York

Other Marshall Cavendish Offices:
Marshall Cavendish International (Asia) Private Limited, 1 New Industrial Road, Singapore 536196 • Marshall Cavendish International (Thailand) Co Ltd. 253 Asoke, 12th Flr, Sukhumvit 21 Road, Klongtoey Nua, Wattana, Bangkok 10110, Thailand • Marshall Cavendish (Malaysia) Sdn Bhd, Times Subang, Lot 46, Subang Hi-Tech Industrial Park, Batu Tiga, 40000 Shah Alam, Selangor Darul Ehsan, Malaysia

Marshall Cavendish is a trademark of Times Publishing Limited

All websites were available and accurate when this book was sent to press.

Library of Congress Cataloging-in-Publication Data
Croy, Anita.
Exploring the Past / by Anita Croy.
p. cm. — (Invisible worlds)
"Describes the hidden artifacts, remains, and other details that help people understand the past"—Provided by publisher.
Includes bibliographical references and index.
ISBN 978-0-7614-4194-6
1. Human remains (Archaeology)—Juvenile literature. 2. Fossils—Juvenile literature.
3. Antiquities, Prehistoric—Juvenile literature. 4. Civilization, Ancient—Juvenile literature. I. Title.
CC79.5.H85C76 2011
930.1—dc22   2009052364

Series created by The Brown Reference Group
www.brownreference.com

For The Brown Reference Group:
Editor: Leon Gray
Designer: Joan Curtis
Picture Managers: Sophie Mortimer and Clare Newman
Picture Researcher: Sean Hannaway
Illustrator: MW Digital Graphics
Managing Editor: Miranda Smith
Design Manager: David Poole
Editorial Director: Lindsey Lowe
Children's Publisher: Anne O'Daly

Consultant: Tim Cooke

Front cover: Science Photo Library/Sinclair Stammers; inset: Shutterstock/Rachelle Burnside

The photographs in this book are used by permission and through the courtesy of:
Alamy: Nathan Benn 41, Blickwinkel 32, Ashley Cooper 38, David Keith Jones/Images of Africa Photobank 31; Corbis: Richard Chung /Reuters 28, Mediscan 39, Ralph White 43–44, Michael S. Yamashita 16; FLPA: Norman Franks 1, 7; Getty Images: Bruno Ferrandez 29, National Geographic 14, Spencer Platt 4–5; PA Photos: Mohammad Al Sehety/AP 36, 37; Rex Features: He Shi 19; Michael Quinn: 10; Science Photo Library: Paul Fisher/North Carolina Museum of Natural Sciences 17, James King-Holmes 23, Philippe Plailly 25, 26, 34, 35, 39, Hubert Raguet/Eurelios 33, Paul Rapson 22, Alexis Rosenfeld 42, Chris Sattleberger 9, Pasquale Sorrentino 20, 21, Jubal Harshaw 13; Shutterstock: Serg64 35 (bottom).

Printed in Malaysia (T)
1 3 5 6 4 2

Contents

Exploring the Past

How do people find out about the past? Most of the information comes from our surroundings. Hidden on or beneath Earth's surface are clues that reveal much about Earth and its inhabitants. Experts might learn from rocks or soil or from the bones of animals and plants that lived in the past.

Many other clues are invisible, but technology can help us find them. For example, tiny particles become visible under a microscope. Techniques such as **radiocarbon dating** help scientists figure out how old something is. Exciting new developments in **genetics** are helping scientists find out how we are related to our ancestors. Science and technology will no doubt continue to help people find out more about the world and its past.

The fossilized remains of this *Tyrannosaurus rex* can reveal useful information about how these dinosaurs used to live.

CHAPTER 1

Record in the Rocks

For a geologist (someone who studies Earth's history through rocks), looking at the different rock layers in a cliff is like reading a history book. The bottom layers are the oldest, while those at the top formed more recently. Layers of rock were often formed by particles of dust settling on the ocean floor. These particles were crushed by more particles above, gradually squeezing them into layers of hard rock. Rocks that once lay deep beneath the oceans have now been pushed high above Earth's surface by the movement of large plates on which Earth's continents lie.

Finding out Earth's age only became possible in the twentieth century, when scientists learned about **radioactivity**. Radiocarbon dating and other dating techniques, such as dating **fossils** in a rock layer, provide a fairly accurate measure of Earth's age and history.

Rocks can also tell us what the weather was like at a particular time. They can also reveal if they were once part of an ocean or land, or whether an area has suffered volcanic eruptions or earthquakes. Rocks hold many secrets. Geologists are learning to unlock those secrets using science and technology.

Layers upon layers of sediment have built up to form this sandstone rock formation in Arizona.

Layers in the Rocks

Earth is made up of five main layers. The inner and outer cores are at Earth's center. Most of the core consists of the metals iron and nickel. The inner core is solid, but the outer core is liquid. The inner and outer mantles are the thick layers of molten rock. The outer mantle is surrounded by a layer of solid rock called the crust. The crust is thin compared to the mantle and core. It is 7 miles (12 kilometers) thick under the oceans and 30 miles (48 km) thick under the continents.

Oceanic crust
7 miles (12 km)

Continental crust
30 miles (48 km)

crust

inner mantle
1,550 miles
(2,480 km)

outer core
1,050 miles
(1,680 km)

outer
mantle
250 miles
(400 km)

inner core
750 miles
(1,200 km)

A cutaway reveals Earth's inner layers—the inner and outer cores, the inner and outer mantles, and the crust.

On the move

The rocks beneath Earth's surface are always on the move, but usually very slowly. Earth's crust is made up of enormous plates of rock, called **tectonic plates**, that slide over the liquid mantle below. Over millions of years, this movement created the huge mountains we can see today. But the same rocks can move very quickly and with terrifying force during an earthquake or a volcano.

Types of rock

There are three different types of rocks: igneous, sedimentary, and metamorphic. **Igneous rocks** form as molten lava cools and hardens. **Sedimentary rocks** are made up of mud, sand, shells, or coral, which settle in layers on Earth's surface. The top layers of mud, sand, shells, and coral push down on the layers below and gradually turn them into rock. **Metamorphic rocks** form when igneous and sedimentary rocks are changed by heat, pressure, or chemical reactions.

Radiocarbon dating

Geologists use radiocarbon dating to date rocks. They measure how quickly radioactive (unstable) elements in the rocks decay (break down) into new elements. The rate of radioactive decay can be used to figure out the age of the rocks.

? Did You Know?

Rocks hide energy in the form of oil and coal. Oil and coal are formed from the remains of animals and plants that lived millions of years ago. The remains become trapped in rocks beneath Earth's surface and slowly turn into oil and coal.

Geologists use special tools to look for oil and coal. The different layers show up in different colors.

A Slice Through Earth's History

The layers of rock in the cliffs of the Grand Canyon are a record of Earth's history. By looking at the rocks, geologists can learn about Earth's past. Over millions of years, the Colorado River has carved a deep **canyon** through the rocks of Arizona. As a result, many layers of rock have been exposed.

Reading rocks

From these layers, and the fossils found within those layers, geologists know that a warm, shallow sea covered the area for more than 600 million years. Then, for some reason, the sea somehow

The Inner Gorge of the Grand Canyon exposes almost two billion years of Earth's geological history.

Close Up

Layers of Precambrian rocks line the bottom of the Inner Gorge. Precambrian rocks date back more than 1.7 billion years. Above these ancient rocks is a layer of Cambrian Tapeats sandstone, which is around 550 million years old. Higher still are layer upon layer of sedimentary rocks, which are between 550 and 250 million years old. There are some gaps in the layers of sedimentary rocks at the top of the Inner Gorge. This reveals that there were periods when no new sediment was laid down or when the earlier sedimentary layers had been eroded away by wind and water.

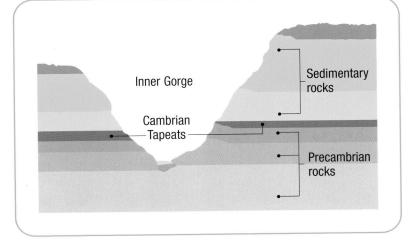

Inner Gorge

Cambrian
Tapeats

Sedimentary
rocks

Precambrian
rocks

vanished and returned many times, leaving mud and sand behind. About ten million years ago, some massive geological force pushed the area up above sea level, resulting in the canyon we see today. The Colorado River still carves its way through the canyon. Erosion by the wind and rain continues to expose rocks and reveal more of Earth's distant past.

Fast Facts

- At its deepest point, the Grand Canyon is 16,000 feet (4,900 meters) deep.

- At its widest point, the Grand Canyon measures 15 miles (25 km) across.

CHAPTER 2

Earliest Life

Earth has been home to life for more than 500 million years. How do we know this? One clue is the fossil record. Fossils are the preserved remains of living things that lived a long time ago.

Living things rot, or decay, when they die. Their bodies are absorbed back into the soil as nutrients for other living things. Sometimes, dead animals or plants are buried in sediment before they start to decay. This also cuts off the oxygen supply, which slows down the rate of decay. As the organism decays slowly, hard parts like bones and teeth are preserved and hardened by minerals in the sediment. Fossils also form when softer body parts, such as organs, decay to leave gaps that are filled by minerals.

The fossil record shows how life-forms have changed over millions of years. By studying these fossils, **paleontologists** (people who study fossils) have been able to study some of the amazing animals and plants that are now extinct. Paleontologists know that the earliest life-forms on Earth were **invertebrates** (animals with backbones). Fossils can also help with dating Earth, because their presence helps to determine the age of the different rock layers.

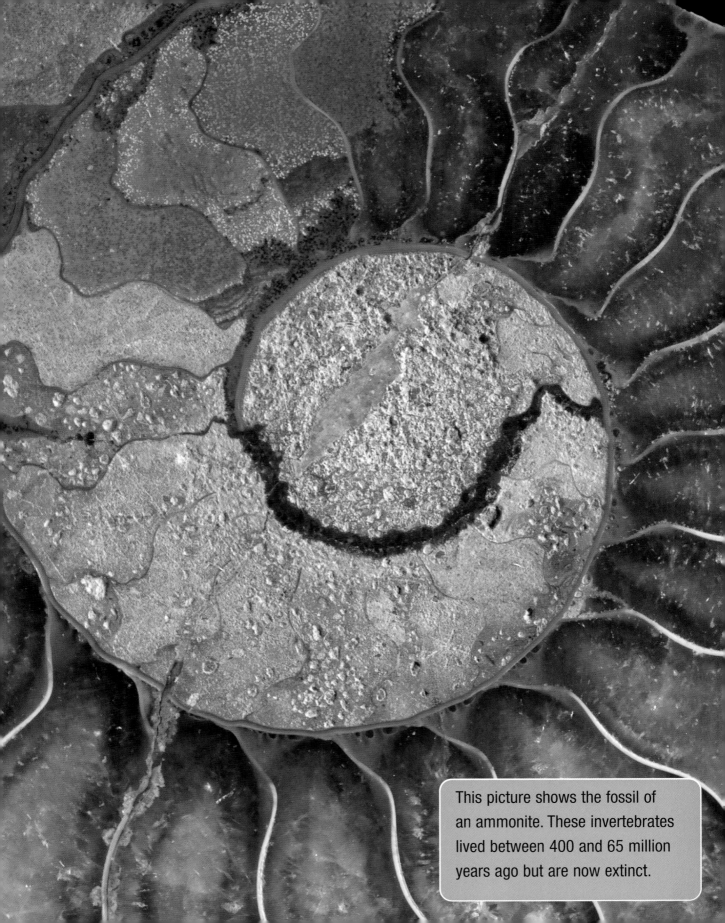

This picture shows the fossil of an ammonite. These invertebrates lived between 400 and 65 million years ago but are now extinct.

Burgess Shale

Fossils such as this trilobite are common at Burgess Shale in Yoho National Park in Canada.

The Burgess Shale reveals an explosion of new life-forms in a very short period of time. There are fossils of all the major groups of animals in the Burgess Shale. Many are still alive today, but many others have long been extinct.

Sitting on top of a mountain ridge in the Canadian Rockies is one of the most amazing discoveries made by paleontologists. The Burgess Shale is famous for the number of fossils found within a small area. Even more remarkably, these fossils date back to the Cambrian Period more than 500 million years ago.

Looking at the past

The Burgess Shale was once hidden beneath the warm, shallow waters of a huge reef on the edge of North America. Every now and then, a huge mudslide from the shore would sweep all the animals to the bottom of the reef and bury them.

Around 175 million years ago, mountains started to form in the area. The reef was forced upward, taking the fossils with it.

The Burgess Shale fossils include soft-bodied marine invertebrates such as brachiopods and mollusks, which appeared about 500 million years ago. There were also many sponges, which are animals that do not move and resemble plants. One of the strangest fossilized animals was a velvet worm. This ancient creature had seven pairs of sharp spines and seven pairs of legs.

? Did You Know?

The most common fossils in the Burgess Shale are those of ammonites. These invertebrates first appeared in the oceans around 400 million years ago. A close relative, *Nautilus*, still lives in the sea today. It has a distinctive outer spiral shell.

This illustration shows the origins of the Burgess Shale and its surroundings as they were around 510 million years ago.

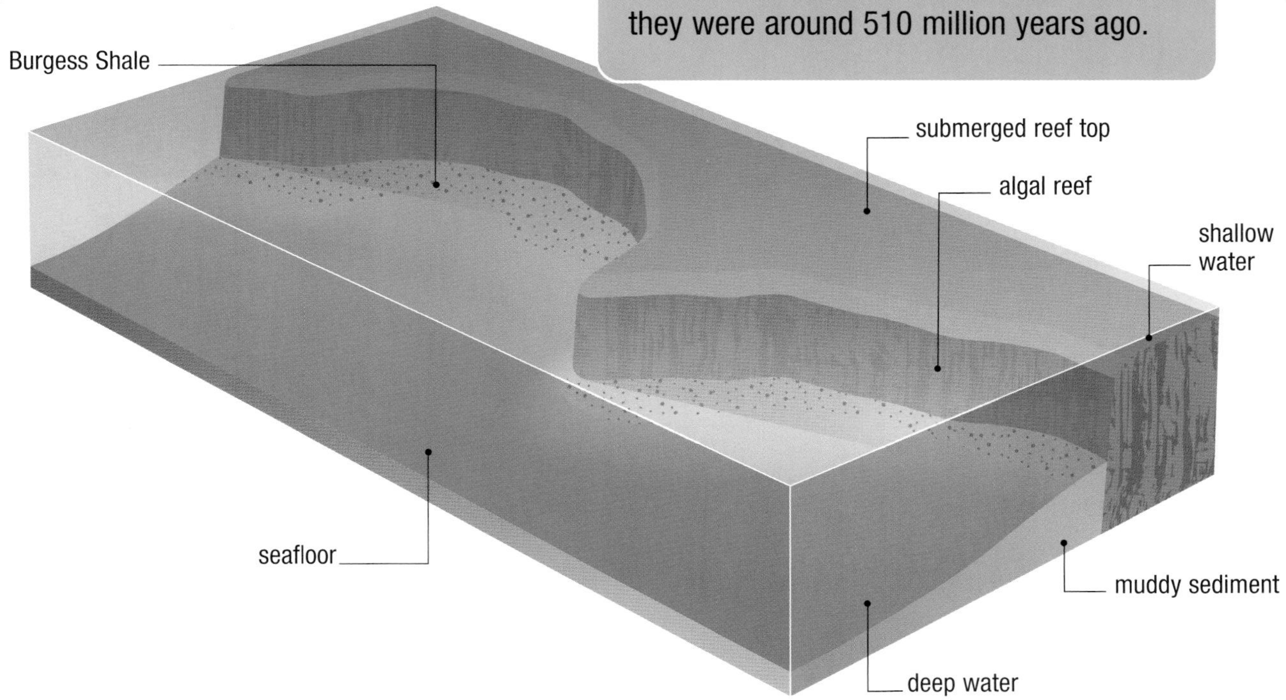

Burgess Shale

submerged reef top

algal reef

shallow water

seafloor

muddy sediment

deep water

Life Evolves

Until two hundred years ago, no one knew that dinosaurs had existed. Then, in 1822, the chance discovery of a giant fossilized tooth changed how we understood Earth's history.

Dr. Gideon Mantell was a fossil collector. Among the collection was a tooth, which was found by Dr. Mantell's wife, Mary Ann Mantell. She soon realized it was unlike any tooth she had seen before. It was clear that the tooth belonged to a big creature that had never been identified. Dr. Mantell had also collected a fossilized footprint. It was almost identical to the print of a lizard called an iguana—but much bigger. Mantell named the creature *Iguanodon*.

The reptile age

The Mantells suggested that the fossils were evidence of large reptiles that were now extinct. The idea set fossil hunters on a

A paleontologist cleans the fossils of a dinosaur called *Albertosaurus* in a laboratory at the Royal Tyrrell Museum, Canada.

new search for more evidence. In the United States, this search started at the same time as the Gold Rush. Prospectors were digging up the ground in search of gold. They also found thousands of large bones. As interest grew, many were taken back to museums and collectors in Europe. In 1842 the huge reptiles were given the name *dinosaur,* or "terrifying lizard."

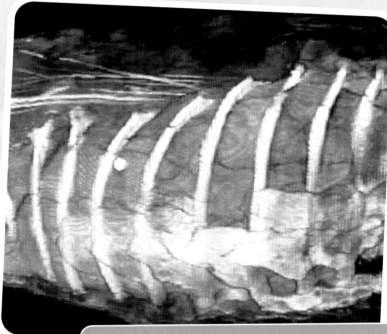

Paleontologists use an imaging technique called **computed tomography** to look at the fossilized internal organs of a dinosaur.

? Did You Know?

One of the ways paleontologists learn about dinosaurs is through coprolites. This is the name for the dinosaurs' fossilized poo. Experts can tell whether they were meat- or plant-eaters by studying coprolites. This helps to show what other kinds of animals and plants existed when the dinosaurs were alive.

Dinosaur discoveries

Since then, the bones of more than 250 dinosaurs have been found. Sometimes, bones from different dinosaurs are found together. The bones come in many different shapes and sizes. It takes special detective work to put them together. Paleontologists are trying to find a way to extract **DNA** from the bones so they can figure out which bones belong to which dinosaur.

CHAPTER 3

Evolution of Humankind

People were shocked when British naturalist Charles Darwin (1809–1882) came up with his idea of evolution and suggested that apes and humans shared a common ancestor. Most experts now agree with Darwin. They think that the earliest human ancestors started to appear in Africa between two and three million years ago. These early ancestors are called **hominids**. One hominid was small, but had a large brain and could make simple stone tools. Experts have given it the name *Homo habilis*.

Homo habilis was thought to be the link between modern humans, *Homo sapiens,* and the older *Australopithecines*. However, experts studying the evolution of humankind do not know for sure. The bones of hominids are very old, and they are often buried deep in sedimentary rocks. It can be hard to know precisely where to look. Often, it is a lucky find that sets the experts on the right path.

Of the few remains that have been found, most are broken skulls or bone fragments. There are no complete skeletons of our earliest ancestors. So the experts can only guess about which species were related and which were not.

Experts find out a lot about human ancestors by studying the remains they leave behind. Bones provide clues about past climates, what people ate, and how they lived.

Examining the Evidence

Archaeologists study fossilized human footprints in volcanic rock near Naples, Italy. The prints date to around 350,000 years ago and were probably made by an early hominid.

It might seem surprising that the remains of our early ancestors have survived millions of years, but they have. A combination of luck and painstaking work by archaeologists has helped uncover them. In some cases, earthquakes and volcanic activity bring to the surface fossils buried deep under the ground. In other cases, millions of years of erosion by wind and water has uncovered them. Some of the most amazing discoveries have been made in Africa. There, archaeologists have found partial skeletons that have revolutionized our understanding of how humankind has evolved.

A scientist studies DNA from the remains of a Peruvian mummy. Because of decay, it is rare to find DNA in ancient remains. In this case, mummification has preserved the DNA.

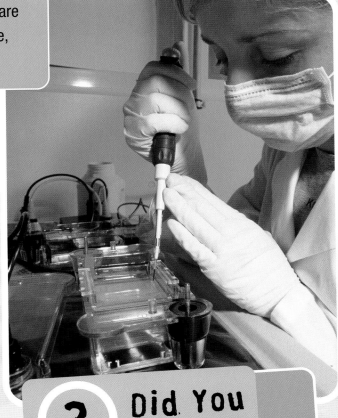

Lucy

"Lucy" is the name given to the partial skeleton of one of our earliest ancestors. Archaeologists found the remains in Ethiopia in 1974. Lucy lived about 3.5 million years ago. She was smaller than an average woman today—about 4 feet (1.3 m) tall. Lucy had many human features, but she was not a human. She may belong to a group of hominids called *Australopithecus*.

Peking Man

"Peking Man" is the name given to a series of fossils found near Beijing (formerly Peking), China, in the 1920s. Experts think that Peking Man is a hominid known as *Homo erectus,* or "upright man"—a direct ancestor of modern humans. It has been very hard to date the fossils. Radiocarbon dating of samples from the site range from 700,000 years to as recently as 13,000 years in age.

? Did You Know?

Deoxyribonucleic acid (DNA) is the molecule that carries the instructions for life. Scientists study DNA from samples taken from substances that are alive or were once alive. DNA is unique, like a fingerprint. In forensic science, it helps identify criminals. In archaeology, it helps show how people are related to their ancestors.

The Toolmakers

Trying to learn about our early ancestors is hard. New discoveries often change scientists' minds. When scientists discovered *Homo habilis* fossils at Olduvai Gorge in East Africa, they realized they had found one of the earliest members of the human family. This new hominid appeared about 2.3 million years ago. Its brain was 50 percent bigger than Lucy's, and its teeth showed that it ate both grass and meat. What made *Homo habilis* really special was its ability to make tools.

Fossil evidence

Fossils showed that *Homo habilis* split stones to make cutting tools. *Homo habilis* may have used wooden tools, too, but the wood has rotted away. Experts know that the tools were used to cut up the bodies of dead animals. There are cut marks on animal bones found at the sites. There are also bite marks on the bones. Some marks were left by *Homo habilis*. Bigger marks were left by the teeth of large carnivores. This indicates that *Homo habilis* was a scavenger, feeding on the remains the carnivores left behind.

A scientist uses a microscope to study a fragment of bone from a hominid skeleton to determine its age and gender.

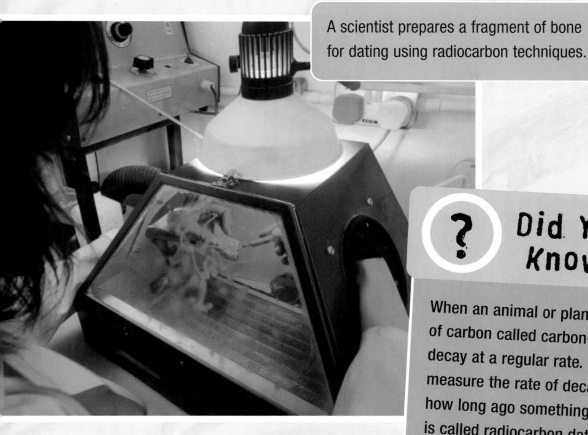

A scientist prepares a fragment of bone for dating using radiocarbon techniques.

? Did You Know?

When an animal or plant dies, a form of carbon called carbon-14 begins to decay at a regular rate. Scientists measure the rate of decay to learn how long ago something died. This is called radiocarbon dating, and it is a useful tool for archaeologists. It can be used to show the age of ancient remains or when trees were cut down to build ancient homes.

Early communities

Eating meat was an important step in the evolution of humankind. If *Homo habilis* did hunt, groups of hunters probably cooperated and shared the kill. Perhaps *Homo habilis* lived in the earliest communities. Toolmaking and hunting are two very challenging activities. This would have helped to speed up the increase in brain size of *Homo habilis*. In turn, a bigger brain would contribute to changes in the body of *Homo habilis*. Our ancestors would need to be more upright to support their bigger heads, so they began to look more like us. Walking upright was also useful to see dangerous predators, allowing our ancestors to defend themselves.

CHAPTER 4

Finding Out About Our Ancestors

Most bodies decay after people die. Most of the remains of ancient people disappear, leaving behind nothing but bones and teeth. When archaeologists are lucky enough to find a body preserved as a **mummy**, it is like getting a glimpse into the past.

Some mummies are preserved by nature. They are found from the frozen mountaintops of Peru to the peat bogs of northern Europe. Other mummies are preserved on purpose. They are found in the deserts of Chile and the pyramids of ancient Egypt. Mummies are exciting finds for archaeologists because advances in technology, such as DNA analysis, radiocarbon dating, and computed tomography (CT) scans, can help them discover a lot of information about the past.

Egyptian archaeologists excavate a burial site to uncover the mummies buried in each chamber.

Skulls, Bones, and Teeth

When a dead body decays, usually only the skeleton and teeth remain. Archaeologists rarely find an entire skeleton. Most of the time they only find partial remains. But that is still helpful. Like a detective investigating a crime, archaeologists can learn a lot from a skull, bones, and teeth.

Teeth are covered with enamel, which is the hardest part of the body. As a result, teeth break down very slowly. Archaeologists can tell a lot about the body from just one tooth. For example, it might

A forensic artist starts to reconstruct the head and face of a woman who lived in Europe in the fifth century.

Close Up

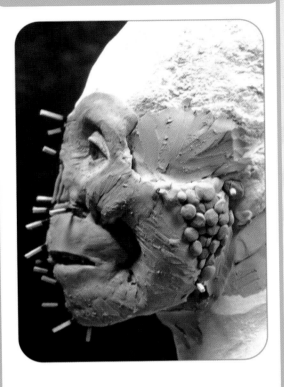

Forensic artists can sometimes recreate a face from someone's skull. This requires a lot of skill. The real skull is carefully protected before a mold is made. The mold is filled with plaster to make a solid cast. The forensic artist uses his or her knowledge of human anatomy to build muscles on the skull. Ideally, any available biographical information about the person will help to create his or her facial expression.

indicate whether the person ate meat, grass, or both. The teeth would be worn away in different ways over the course of a lifetime. With more recent remains, teeth can reveal more about a person's life. Did the person smoke a pipe? A groove worn into a tooth might prove that he or she did.

Skeleton secrets

The shape of the skull has helped archaeologists determine the link between early *Homo habilis* and modern *Homo sapiens*. Borrowing a technique from forensic crime labs, experts use skulls to recreate the faces. This can show us how our ancestors looked.

The length of bones in the body can reveal how old a person was, whether he or she was male or female, and if he or she was healthy or sick. Broken bones may indicate an accident or even how they died. Lab tests show what diseases the person had.

DNA and radiocarbon dating tests determine a person's genetic makeup and age. DNA also indicates whether individuals were related.

X rays of Mummies

Archaeologists study the X ray of a 3,000-year-old Egyptian mummy.

When archaeologists found the first mummies, they did not realize what a rich supply of information they had. In 1922, British archaeologist Howard Carter (1874–1939) found the mummy of Egyptian **pharaoh** Tutankhamun in Egypt. Carter simply unwrapped the mummy to look inside! Today, archaeologists

? Did You Know?

Tutankhamun died young. He was buried quickly in a simple tomb. A recent CT scan found a wound in the pharaoh's thigh. He may have had an accident and then died from his injury, or maybe he was murdered.

Close Up

Since contact with air can damage a mummy, archaeologists use X rays to study preserved human remains without damaging them. Computed tomography (CT) involves taking X rays from different angles. A computer then builds them into a 3D picture. For example, a CT scan of the mummy of a pharaoh named Seramon revealed a scarab necklace under the wrappings.

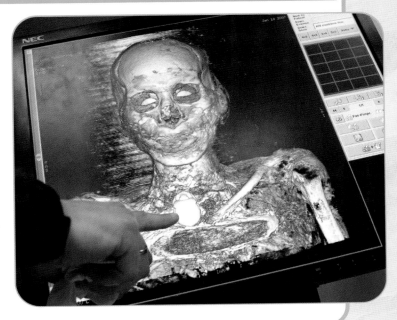

know to protect the mummies from the air. Instead, they use **X rays** to look at the remains.

Juanita

Desert heat, ice, and peat bogs have preserved bodies in ways similar to the ancient Egyptians. The frozen remains of a mummy named Juanita were found on the slopes of a volcano in Peru. Radiocarbon tests showed she died about 500 years ago. Tests have shown that Juanita ate vegetables six hours before she died from a blow to the side of her head. Experts think that she may have been killed as a sacrifice to the Inca gods.

Buried in the bog

Archaeologists have found many preserved bodies in the peat bogs of northern Europe. They span a wide period of time. Radiocarbon dating has shown the age of many of these finds. Their stomach contents have also been analyzed to find out what they ate for their last meal.

CHAPTER 5

Hidden Homes

Our early ancestors lived in caves. Archaeologists have found bones hidden in the caves. The bones tell us what sort of animals our ancestors ate. Paintings on the walls show how they hunted. As civilizations grew, caves and mud huts gave way to stone cities. But even large cities vanish over many centuries. They might be covered by sand or sea, hidden under a big rain forest, or buried under more recent buildings. But these settlements never disappear completely.

Sometimes, ancient homes reappear by chance. A construction worker digging foundations might find a piece of brick in the soil. Archaeologists come to investigate, and the brick might lead them to discover an ancient city. This was how the ancient Aztec capital of Teotihuacán was discovered under the Central Plaza in Mexico City. In Britain, experts can trace back the development of London to Roman times by digging down through the layers of soil and debris.

Whenever a large site is cleared for construction in a major city, archaeologists will usually be called in to catalog any ancient finds. They are able to record the past and learn more before building begins.

A staircase leads down to the underground burial chamber of the pharaoh Khufu (Cheops) at the Great Pyramid near Cairo, Egypt.

Patterns in the Ground

One of the best ways to see what lies beneath the ground is to look at it from above. The military used aerial photography to study the enemy during World War 1 (1914–1918) and World War II (1939–1945). The pilots noticed that they could also see the shape of the land beneath them.

Sky high

Aerial photography is now a routine part of archaeology. At the end of the day, when the Sun creates long shadows, archaeologists fly low over an area and take photos facing into the Sun. The combination of sunshine and shadows reveals unevenness in the land. The photos might show the outlines of houses or tracks, or a ditch that once surrounded an ancient building. Other details, invisible from ground level, will also become apparent.

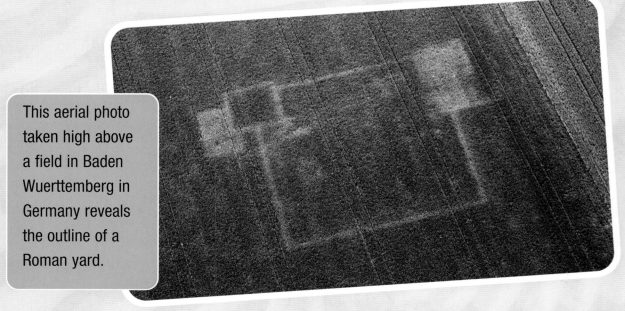

This aerial photo taken high above a field in Baden Wuerttemberg in Germany reveals the outline of a Roman yard.

An archaeologist studies infrared aerial photographs of a site.

Aerial photography can reveal a site beneath a field of crops. Crops grow taller when there is plenty of water in the roots. If something is buried beneath the roots, it may stop the crops from growing as tall as neighboring crops. So variations in crop height could mean that an object is buried in the ground.

Invisible light

Archaeologists use thermal imaging and **infrared** photography to learn more about sites. They both work by detecting disturbances in the land.

Thermal imaging measures tiny changes in the temperature of the land. Infrared is similar to an X ray of what lies beneath the surface.

? Did You Know?

Archaeologists study the soil to learn about sites. Small disturbances in soil changes how vegetation grows. Thermal imaging reveals differences between the soil types.

Digs and Trenches

Modern archaeologists excavate a site in a careful and organized way. Before they begin, they think about the questions they want to answer, for example, "When was this site built?" or "Why was it abandoned?" Then they start to dig. First, they divide the site into small squares, called quadrants, using string. This makes it easier to record the positions of all the things they find.

An archaeologist uses a laptop to survey the site of an early Christian church in Arles, France.

The dig

There are two major parts to a dig. First, archaeologists dig a trench across the site. The trench reveals the different layers in the ground and any objects buried within them. The most recent layers are closer to the surface, and the oldest are at the bottom of the trench. The trench is usually quite long and deep and wide enough for archaeologists to climb in and examine the layers.

If the trench reveals something hidden in the earth, archaeologists begin a dig. This uncovers a larger area to reveal the horizontal layout of the site—perhaps to show the outline of a building or maybe a whole city.

Science of archaeology

Modern archaeologists know that where an object is found can be as important as what it is. It might reveal the purpose of a particular

Close Up

Modern archaeologists rely on computers to find out more about the sites they are studying. The archaeologist on the left is making a detailed survey of the site of a church in Arles, France, using a laptop. He can then feed the data directly into his main computer back at the laboratory (right). The archaeologist has used the data to build a computer reconstruction of the church complex as it would have looked in the fourth century, when the Romans built it.

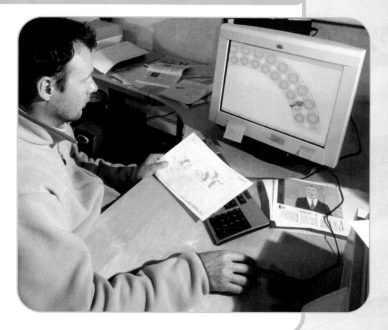

room in a house, for example. Where an object is found in the ground can also help to date it. Dendrochronology and radiocarbon dating can also help to tell the age of an object. Such clues all add to our knowledge of past civilizations.

If you cut down some types of trees you will see that the trunk has a lot of rings.

? Did You Know?

Dendrochronology is the science of tree rings. The rings allow experts to tell the tree's age. One ring usually equals one year's growth. Experts know how wet or dry a year was from the width of a ring. This shows what it was like at the time.

Looking Inside Structures

The pyramids were tombs for the Egyptian pharaohs. The tomb builders did not want the dead pharaohs to be disturbed. And they did not want anyone to be able to steal the treasures buried inside the tombs. So the builders constructed the pyramids with sealed entrances, secret tunnels, and dead ends. Even though the pyramids are the world's most famous monuments, we know very little about what is inside them—or even how they were built. Archaeologists are now using new technologies, such as robotic cameras, to find out more about these secret tombs.

Stonehenge

Another famous ancient site is also shrouded in mystery. No one knows why people erected the huge stones

Archaeologists use a robotic camera to explore deep inside the Great Pyramid of Khufu (Cheops) near Cairo, Egypt.

at Stonehenge, England. One idea is that it is an "ancient computer" to track the stars. Aerial photography and advances in surveying are revealing new information. We know that that the stones have been moved from their original position. Some have disappeared. None of those details are visible to the naked eye.

Look inside

Archaeologists use other new techniques to see inside things that seem to be solid. They study electrical currents or magnetic fields or use ground-penetrating **radio waves** (radar) to learn more about new archaeological sites.

Close Up

The Great Pyramid of Khufu (Cheops) was built around 4,500 years ago. Deep inside the pyramid are two burial chambers. Each chamber can be reached by a small, steep tunnel. Smaller shafts lead upward from each burial chamber. They are too small for people to squeeze through, but archaeologists have used robotic cameras to explore them.

The robotic cameras also recorded pictures of a sealed stone door in one of the shafts that led from the "Queen's Chamber." When a robotic camera was

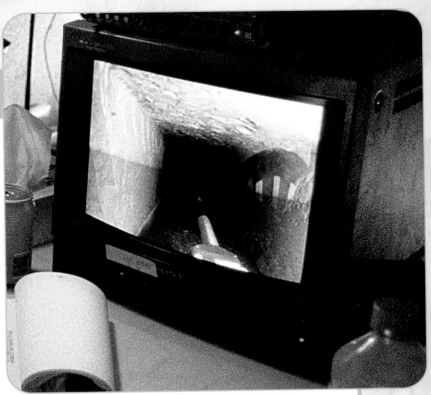

inserted through a hole drilled in the "door," it revealed yet another stone door. The archaeologists still do not know if there is anything beyond that door. The pyramid still might have secrets to reveal!

Middens and Pollens

One of the best places to find clues about how our ancestors lived is in **middens**—the archaeologist's term for a trash heap.

Trash can tell us a lot about the past: what people ate, what they did, and how they lived. Discarded bones reveal what types of animals were eaten for food. Fragments of ceramic show that people could make pots and may indicate what they were used for.

Under the microscope

Some of the most useful clues found in middens cannot be seen by the naked eye. Cooking pots or the pits used to store food often contain ancient **pollen**—the tiny particles that plants use to make new plants. Archaeologists study pollen under a powerful electron microscope. The tiny grains can reveal a lot of useful information. For example, archaeologists know how Earth's climate has changed over the last two and a half million years by looking at pollen records and comparing them to deposits of plants buried beneath the sea.

Middens are a potential goldmine of information for archaeologists.

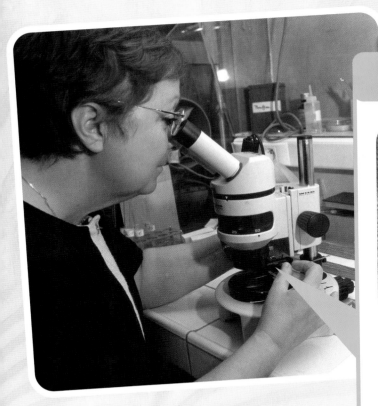

Pollen science

Pollen is useful because it does not decay. Every plant has its own type of pollen. **Palynologists** (scientists who study pollen) can tell what types of plants were growing at a particular time by studying ancient pollen grains. This provides clues about the climate and environment. Archaeologists also know what types of crops people grew and how they ate them. Pollen samples from soil tell them about the local vegetation. Pollen found in bogs and lakes can tell archaeologists more about the plants growing over a wider area.

When palynologists study soil samples under a microscope, the tiny pollen grains show up in many different shapes and sizes. Most pollen grains range in size from about 15 to 100 **microns**. The palynologist can identify the plant from the unique shape and size of the pollen and the markings on its surface.

Fossilized pollen grains have also shown how plants have evolved since they first began to diversify during the Cretaceous Period—a period in Earth's history between 145 and 65 million years ago.

CHAPTER 6

Buried Treasures

When hikers stumbled across the frozen body of a man in the Austrian Alps in 1991, criminal investigators were called to the scene. They wanted to identify the corpse and check that the death was not suspicious. They were in for a big surprise—the man went missing more than five thousand years before. Archaeologists did many tests on the frozen remains, but it was the objects found close to his body that helped date Ötzi, as he was nicknamed. Archaeologists dated Ötzi's dagger to the Copper Age, which lasted from 4000 BCE to around 3000 BCE.

Earlier, in 1939, archaeologists discovered a ship buried beneath a mound at Sutton Hoo in Britain. The burial took place around the seventh century CE. The many treasures in the grave included a spectacular silver bowl that had been made by Byzantine craftsmen.

Archaeologists can learn a lot from the everyday objects they find at sites. For example, they might find old stone tools or bits of pottery when a field is plowed. These objects may not be valued as treasures, but they are extremely valuable to archaeologists who are trying to find out about the past.

This gold and silver treasure was found buried in the royal tomb of the Lord of Sipán in northern Peru.

Finding Artifacts

It is not only experts who find ancient sites and valuable objects. Many of the most amazing archaeological discoveries have been found by accident. Farmers plowing their fields have also found important items. In fact, anyone can search for buried treasure. The invention of the metal detector has helped many hobbyists make some important discoveries.

Metal detectives

The sensitivity of the detector depends on the model. Some of the most sensitive and more expensive models can find metal objects buried deep underground. On a professional dig, a detector is just one of many tools that help archaeologists find buried **artifacts** at a site. Detectors used

An amateur archaeologist uses a metal detector to scan the seafloor in search of metal treasures.

by hobbyists are better at finding metal nearer the surface. Most detectors can find metal buried at a depth of up to 12 inches (30 cm). This depends on the size of the object and the type of metal. Even so, hobbyists have made some amazing finds. In England, metal detectors have found old coins that date back to the Roman and Viking times. But amateur archaeologists need to work as carefully as the professionals, so that they do not destroy evidence as they dig.

? Did You Know?

At Sutton Hoo, large mounds of earth concealed treasures that belonged to an Anglo Saxon king who ruled in England in the seventh century. The treasures included silver and gold helmets, a solid gold buckle, gold shoulder clasps, solid silver bowls, a silver plate, and many gold coins.

Close Up

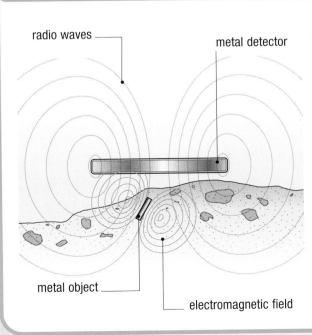

radio waves

metal detector

metal object

electromagnetic field

Archaeologists and amateurs alike use a metal detector to look for anything made from metal or with metal in it. Metal detectors will locate valuable metal objects such as coins and jewelry, as well as scrap metal and even rocks with a high metal content. The detector uses radio waves to scan for metal. When the radio waves hit metal in the ground, an electromagnetic field is generated. An antenna in the detector picks up this field and sets off an alarm.

Underwater Archaeology

Robert Ballard and his team of marine archaeologists found these china dishes among the debris left from the wreck of the *Titanic*.

Most of Earth's surface is covered by water, so it makes sense that many objects must be lying on the bottom of rivers, seas, and oceans waiting to be found. Some things, such as wood, keep better under the water than on dry land. Metal objects also survive, but they become covered in mineral deposits.

Once objects are removed from the water, they need special care to keep them in good condition.

People who study underwater sites such as shipwrecks are called marine archaeologists. Shipwrecks are an extremely valuable source of information about life in the past. The contents, as well as the ship,

? Did You Know?

The *Titanic* sank on its maiden voyage from England to New York in 1912. In 1985, a team led by Robert Ballard began to search the area where the *Titanic* had sunk. They used TV cameras mounted on a special sled to find the ship. The next year they returned with a submersible to travel down to the wreck. Many artifacts have since been brought to the surface.

Conclusion

People have been studying the past for centuries, but it has only been in the last two hundred years that their work has become the science that we know today. Modern archaeologists and paleontologists are using science and technology to unlock the secrets of the past. They use technologies from radiocarbon dating to determine age to electron microscopy to look at objects in incredibly fine detail.

Archaeologists and paleontologists are a bit like history detectives. Their job is to piece together a story from the few fragments of evidence that our ancestors and ancient plants and animals left behind. The evidence could be valuable treasures at the bottom of the ocean or fossils buried deep underground. Thanks to the efforts of these detectives, we now know much more about the past than before. But the hidden remains of the past continue to be found. Who knows what what else will be discovered or revealed in the future?

can tell archaeologists a lot about the time in history when they sank.

Marine archaeology has developed quickly in the past fifty years. The development of **submersibles** and SCUBA gear have made it possible for archaeologists to stay underwater for long enough to carry out proper excavations of important sites.

Glossary

artifact An artifact is an object made by ancient people and later found by archaeologists.

canyon A canyon is a long, narrow valley with steep cliffs.

computed tomography In computed tomography, a computer combines many X ray images to build up a picture, called a CT scan, of the insides of the body.

DNA Short for deoxyribonucleic acid, DNA molecules contain the instructions for life.

fossil A fossil is the remains or the impression of an animal or plant that lived a long time ago.

genetics Genetics is a branch of biology that studies how parents pass on characteristics to their offspring.

hominids The early ancestors of modern human beings are called hominids.

igneous rock Igneous rock such as granite forms when lava cools and hardens.

infrared Hot objects give off a type of radiation called infrared.

invertebrate An invertebrate is an animal that lacks a backbone.

metamorphic rock Metamorphic rock such as slate forms when existing rock changes under the action of heat and pressure.

micron One micron is one millionth of a meter.

midden A midden is an ancient trash heap, often containing bones, shells, and broken pots.

mummy A mummy is a body preserved by nature (such as freezing in ice) or on purpose (by wrapping it in bandages).

paleontologist A paleontologist studies the remains of ancient life.

palynologist A palynologist studies the pollen and spores of plants.

pharaoh An ancient Egyptian king was called a pharaoh.

pollen Plants use tiny particles called pollen to make new plants.

radioactivity Radioactivity occurs when unstable elements break down to form new elements.

radiocarbon dating Scientists use this technique to figure out the age of things by measuring their radioactive decay.

radio waves This type of radiation sends and receives signals.

sedimentary rock Sedimentary rock such as sandstone forms as pieces of rock slowly press down on the layers below.

submersible An underwater vessel called a submersible is used by scientists to explore the depths of the ocean.

tectonic plate A tectonic plate is a rigid piece of Earth's crust.

X ray An X ray is an energetic form of light.

Find Out More

Books

Arato, Rona. *Fossils: Clues to Ancient Life.* New York: Crabtree Publishing Company, 2004.

Barnes, Trevor, and Tony Robinson. *Archaeology.* New York: Kingfisher, 2007.

Earth's History. Edited by Jacqueline A. Ball. New York: Gareth Stevens Publishing, 2004.

Halls, Kelly Milner. *Mysteries of the Mummy Kids.* Plain City, Ohio: Darby Creek Publishing, 2007.

Sloan, Christopher. *The Human Story: Our Evolution from Prehistoric Ancestors to Today.* National Geographic Children's Books, 2004.

Websites

http://education.usgs.gov/
Visit the website of the United States Geological Survey to find out how science can help us understand our changing world.

http://www.becominghuman.org/
Explore the origins of humankind at the Becoming Human website. Click on the "Launch the Documentary" to watch a documentary that takes you through four million years of human evolution.

http://www.digonsite.com/
Visit the website of the magazine *dig*™ to explore the science of archaeology. Test your knowledge with fun quizzes and contests.

http://www.paleoportal.org/
Find out all about fossils at the Paleontology Portal. Click on the "K–12" link for more websites you can visit for more information.

Index

Page numbers in **boldface** are illustrations.